The Ab Snowman

Written by John Parsons
Illustrated by Peter Townsend

Rigby

The Abominable
Snowman

With these characters ...

Orville
O'Leary

Orville's
Mother

The
Abominable
Snowman

The
Scientists

"Our task: to hunt for

Mount Everest is the highest mountain in the world. High in the snow-covered mountains nearby, three scientists and an explorer are hunting for the mysterious Abominable Snowman. But all their scientific equipment doesn't help them — even though the Abominable Snowman is close.
Very close!

the Abominable Snowman ..."

Chapter 1.

Orville O'Leary is an explorer. He shivered as he looked up at Mount Everest.
A photo of his mother was beside him.

But Orville wasn't thinking about his mother. He was thinking about what to write in his explorer's diary. His hunt for the mysterious Abominable Snowman had started.

Day 1

We are camping on the snow-covered slopes of Mount Everest. Our camp is surrounded by massive mountains. Our task is to hunt for the mystery Abominable Snowman. People say they have seen it here. But no scientist has ever seen one!

 With my three scientists, we will
find out if the Abominable Snowman
lives here. We will use our scientific
equipment to help us keep watch all
day and all night. If the Abominable
Snowman comes close to our camp,
we will be watching.

Our supplies will last for one month.
There are noodles to eat, bottles of root
beer to drink, and soap to wash with.
And much, much more! We will not be
hungry or thirsty.

Chapter 2

Day 2

My morning water is icy cold. It's so cold that when my nose dribbled, the dribbles turned into icicles.

My team of scientists have set up video cameras around the camp. If the Abominable Snowman comes close, we will record it on video.

Today, we talked about and drew what the Abominable Snowman might look like. It has to keep warm, so it must have thick fur. It could be fat, as humans and animals store energy in their fat. It may have huge, flat feet to help it walk across snow. Everyone now knows to look out for a large furry creature with huge feet!

Day 3

This morning we got very excited.
A large furry creature with huge feet
was spotted. We pounced on it!

Unfortunately, it was my mother!
I felt so embarrassed.

I keep telling her that I'm old enough to take care of myself. But she *still* follows me around when I'm working and exploring.

Fortunately, she brought more clean clothes and blankets for me.

Chapter 3

Day 4

Today we are trying to attract the Abominable Snowman by leaving food out as bait. We left out lots of chocolate and other sweets. However, the video camera recorded my mother eating all the chocolate last night. Now we are using *her* as bait!

Day 5

We forgot to bring Mother in last night. She was very happy to see us when we found her buried up to her neck in snow.

The Abominable Snowman didn't eat Mother last night. Maybe it doesn't like people. Could it be a vegetarian?

Still we have not spotted one. I begin to think that it might not exist.

Mother says that we are not eating enough healthy food. We tell her that we have five flavors of noodles. But when we went to show her, we saw that five packs of noodles were missing.

We checked our video recordings, but there was no Abominable Snowman to be seen. Mother still wants us to eat more healthy food, like vegetables.

We agreed to eat vegetables, but only if they are on a pizza. Mother knows a pizza place that delivers for free. She used her mobile phone to order vegetarian pizzas.

Chapter 4.

Day 20

Our pizzas arrived — finally! But
Mother forgot to tell us the pizza place
was in Australia! The pizzas were cold
and smelled disgusting. But, after
20 days of eating noodles, we ate
them anyway.

The pizza man rode away, covered in snow.

We still haven't sighted the Abominable Snowman. We have been camping here for almost a month. If we do not see one soon, we will have to believe that it does not exist.

Day 31

On the last day of the month, we heard some strange news on the radio. Some people in Australia have seen a strange, fat, flat-footed furry creature on a beach. I told the scientists to pack up the equipment and what was left of our supplies.

We're leaving the Abominable Snowman and this cold, icy place right now! We're heading for the hot, sunny beaches of Australia. We're going to hunt for an even more exciting creature . . .

"Where Can You Be?"

Abominable Snowman, this is our mission:
We're looking for you on an expedition!
Abominable Snowman, where can you be?
Abominable Snowman, why can't we see
What you are doing or what you look like?
Is it because you left on a red motorbike?